Charlene Marshall

CHARLENE MARSHALL
MY EXTRAORDINARY ODYSSEY
A MEMOIR

by Vonnetta Mayo

Charlene Marshall

Copyright © 2023 by Vonnetta Mayo

All rights reserved

No portion of this book may be reproduced, stored in a retrieval system, or transmitted in any form by any means–electronic, mechanical, photocopy, recording, or other–except for brief quotations in printed reviews, without prior permission of the author.

First Edition

Library of Congress Control Number: 2022921749

This book is dedicated to my late husband, Rogers Leon Marshall Sr., and my late son, Rogers Leon Marshall Jr. May they always be remembered and hold a special place in my heart.

Love always!
Charlene Marshall

CONTENTS

"Florist" Family	1
1. The Mines	5
2. The Marshalls	10
3. Political Awareness	19
4. Marshall's Law	27
5. Elected Official	38
6. Rebirth and Regrowth	45
7. My Journey	56
Final Destination	64

"FLORIST" FAMILY

One afternoon, I was walking down the street in Morgantown, West Virginia, and a young lady approached me. She asked me whether I had a job and whether I would like to work at a florist shop. I had never seen this lady before. But she said she had noticed my smile and how I spoke to everybody. Even though I didn't know this lady, I responded, "Yes, I have a part-time job."

She asked, "Would you like to have another job?"

"Sure," I replied.

At the time, I was sixteen years old, but I had been working since I was twelve. Back then, families would call high schools, talk to the secretaries, and ask whether any young ladies wanted to work after school. So I would often volunteer to work after school. I worked for many families throughout the area. Whether it was babysitting or other odd little domestic jobs, I was always doing something. My stepfather sometimes would tease me and say, "People are going to think *you're* raising a family." And I would just laugh.

This lady, whose name I found out was Jean, went up the street to the florist shop, and I happily followed her. Later, I found out that she worked there.

When we arrived at the florist shop, I met the Batlas family—Mr. Batlas, the owner of Morgantown Florist Company, and his two sons. It was the older son who hired me. My duties included cleaning and arranging the funeral floral arrangements. Every day before school, I would come and clean the floors.

I would always bring my lunch to work because finding a place to eat back then was hard. I remember looking at the back of a Hunt's tomato sauce recipe book where I saw a recipe for lasagna and thinking, *I can't wait until I'm able to go into a restaurant and eat lasagna.* Wherefore, I will never forget how excited I was about going to this restaurant on High Street; it was renowned for having the best sandwiches. When I arrived at the restaurant's counter, I ordered a sandwich to go. As I waited anxiously at the counter for my order, other customers were coming in. They were being seated and having their orders taken. As more time elapsed, I grew more anxious. I noticed the customers who had come in after me were receiving their food at their tables. I was humiliated! I thought, *I will never put myself in this position again.* After about forty-five minutes, I received my order. When I left that restaurant, my appetite for that sandwich, sadly, left too.

However, the Batlas family was always very nice to me. One day, they noticed I didn't have anywhere to eat, so they invited me upstairs to eat with them. They were Greek and had Greek dishes served on the table. There I tasted some of their Greek dishes. After that, eating together became our normal routine. That was just the first of many nice gestures the Batlas family extended to me.

"Florist" Family

My best friend was Annette Chandler. We graduated high school together. After integration, Annette Chandler became the first African American woman to receive an undergraduate degree from West Virginia University. She and I loved to get sundaes from Dairy Queen and walk around. One afternoon, the older Batlas brother, who had hired me, saw us and asked, "Why are you walking in the street?" That upset him. He couldn't figure out why we were walking up and down the street.

I wondered, *Why is he so upset?* We were enjoying window shopping. Looking at all the clothes and the jewelry through the windows was fun for us.

Nevertheless, they were getting ready to go to the movies at the Metropolitan Theatre. So he asked us whether we wanted to go to the movies with them. We said, "Sure." He bought us tickets to a movie. It was a comedy. I wasn't always crazy about comedy. But that was the first time I saw Dean Martin and Jerry Lewis. Even though we viewed the movie from the balcony, it still was an unforgettable moment.

Thereafter, the Batlas family became my extended family. They were always looking out for my well-being, even sometimes purchasing my school supplies. I'm delighted to say that the Batlas family played an essential role in my upbringing.

I remember when the older Batlas brother married his wife, Irene. Irene was a schoolteacher at Morgantown Junior High School. She had such a beautiful spirit and was always very kind to me. I'm so grateful that I had the opportunity to meet her.

I have been privileged to see three generations of the Batlas family. Mr. Batlas, who was the owner of Morgantown Florist Company, had a granddaughter who lived here in Cheat Lake, West Virginia. When I had the opportunity to meet her, she told me she had heard the story about how I met and worked for her grandfather. I thought, *As peculiar the way that I met them was, I'm grateful to have had the opportunity to meet the Batlas family.*

Jean, who saw me walking down the street in Morgantown and asked me whether I wanted to work at a florist shop, worked at the florist shop for years. I never asked her why she chose me. I just figured she saw a happy Black girl and thought, *Maybe she'll like to work at a florist shop.*

Who knew later I would acquire most of my elected positions in an unprecedented way?

ONE
THE MINES

I WAS BORN IN 1933, and I believe my father, Charlie Jennings, wanted a boy. He named me Charlene, after him. I am the third oldest: I had five sisters and one brother. My father was a coal miner, and my mother was a stay-at-home mom. Born and raised in Osage, West Virginia, which is also known as Scotts Run, I attended Floyd B. Cox School from first through sixth grade. From seventh through twelfth grade, I attended Monongalia High School in Westover, West Virginia. During that time, it was the only high school in the county that Blacks were allowed to attend. At Monongalia High, I won the "Ms. Monongalia" title. At that time, the Monongalia High basketball team defeated the Kelly Miller High basketball team, the all-Black school in Clarksburg, West Virginia, in the state championship. In addition, I was voted at Monongalia High as the person who participated in the most activities. As I mentioned before, I was always doing something.

Though I didn't attend the same schools as the white children, after school, we all still played together. We played kickball in the street. And when it snowed, we rode our sleds down the hills together. Everybody in Osage was equal. It was a very diverse population. My neighbors consisted of all nationalities. Therefore, we didn't know the difference until we went to school.

Osage is in rural Monongalia County. It was a coal mining town. Coal cars ran on the railroad tracks alongside the streets. As a result, Osage was frowned upon by other cities in Monongalia County. It was considered substandard.

Yet I enjoyed growing up there. It was fun. Everyone was nice. We did the best we could with what we had. Moreover, my father mined at the coal camp near Morgantown at Osage #3. Everyone's dad looked the same, covered in coal dust when he came out of the maw of the mine at the end of his shift.

Unfortunately, one day my father didn't come out of the mine. He was killed in the mine when I was six years old. At that time, I had four sisters and one brother. And my mother, Christine, whom everyone knew as "Missie," quickly became the breadwinner. It was *rough*! In that era, there were not many job options for women. So my siblings and I had to contribute and help out with things around the house. It was a very troubling time in my life, though. I remember going to my father's closet and smelling his shirts that were hanging up simply because I *missed him so much*!

I also recall following my father around like a puppy as a child. When he was home, I would tag along with him wherever he went. And I'd be talking the whole time. I wouldn't leave him alone even for a second. When he went outside to chop wood for our potbelly stove, I would be there to help him carry the wood inside. Helping my father carry wood and working from an early age is where I believe my work ethic developed.

When my father passed away, the widow's benefits were only $30 a month and $5 extra a month for each child in the household. Later, those benefits went up after the United Mine Workers of America started raising hell. That's when I started paying attention to unions.

Nonetheless, about five years after my father passed, "Missie" remarried. My stepfather, Ollie Cranford, was great. He was always teasing me about having multiple jobs. Additionally, he and my mother conceived a child. Now I had five sisters and one brother. Our family was growing, and everything seemed great.

Meanwhile, I was off to college. But I couldn't attend college in Monongalia County. It was 1952, and West Virginia University didn't accept Black undergraduate students. So I had to travel to the opposite end of the state to attend Bluefield State College, an all-Black college. There I pursued an education degree. And while I was there, I stayed with my former Monongalia High School principal, Mr. Anderson, and his wife. They lived in Bluefield, West Virginia, and were nice enough to give me room and board.

But after I had spent about one year at Bluefield State College, my studies were cut short. My stepfather, just like my father and grandfather, was killed in a mining accident. He was killed in a cave-in. And my grandfather had been killed in a mine when my mother was a child. This was a *tragedy*! I was deeply saddened by his loss. And I couldn't imagine how my mother was feeling. She lost two husbands and a father to the mines. Sadly, she and my stepfather had been married for only four years when he passed.

Yet again, my mother became our sole provider. My mother's unconditional love was astonishing. She didn't say it. She showed it! She was a strong woman who always put her children first. She would say, "You work hard for your kids because your kids are everything." She also did her best to help others when she could.

However, regrettably, after my stepfather passed, my family could no longer afford my college tuition. It would have been tremendous savings financially if I had been able to attend West Virginia University. But Brown v. Board of Education, the Supreme Court ruling that US state laws establishing racial segregation in public schools are unconstitutional, even if the segregated schools are otherwise equal in quality, wasn't decided until 1954. That would give all the youth equal opportunities because the schools were not equal. The classes and the equipment weren't either.

Still, as usual, my mother, my siblings, and I persevered through this difficult time. Then eventually, all my siblings moved away. Some of my sisters moved to New Jersey, and some of them moved to Ohio. Unfortunately, my brother was killed in an auto accident. Therefore, my mother and I were the only ones who stayed in Osage as I couldn't imagine going anywhere else. And my mother would have had to be forced to leave Osage. Even then, she would have put up a fight.

Nevertheless, my mother and I missed my siblings tremendously. But we communicated with them regularly. They would call and talk to us on the phone for hours. And when they came home to visit, it would be like old times again. We would all sit around and talk about the fun times we had growing up in Osage. Then my sisters and I would laugh uncontrollably.

I also visited them in New Jersey and Ohio. Seeing new places is fun. Furthermore, during the era of segregation, there was a book originated and published by Victor H. Green, an African American mailman in New York City, titled *The Negro Motorist Green-Book*, also known as the *Green Book*. It was an annual guidebook for African American travelers. It listed places throughout North America, such as hotels and restaurants, that were safe for African Americans to travel to.

I really like New Jersey. It's fun going to the Amish markets and buying their meats and spices. Therefore, I enjoyed every visit! Yet I still couldn't wait to get back home to Osage. To me, there was no place like home.

TWO
THE MARSHALLS

Surprisingly, I moved from Osage to Morgantown, West Virginia, in 1952 when I married my husband, Rogers Leon Marshall. The distance between the two areas is only about eight minutes. Rogers and his family already resided in Morgantown, and he and I met in junior high school. His parents, Mr. and Mrs. Marshall, lived at 457 White Avenue. So Rogers and I bought a home in the city's Greenmont neighborhood on White Avenue. It was downtown with a diverse population that reminded me of home.

Mr. and Mrs. Marshall were renowned for providing room and board to West Virginia University African American students. Before Brown v. Board of Education, African American graduate students were allowed to attend WVU, but they were not allowed to stay on campus or in the dorms. In addition, educators from all over the world would come into town for workshops. They would stay with other families, but they would make reservations to have their meals at the Marshalls' home. Therefore, 457 White Avenue became a hangout spot for many African American students and educators. As a result, a lot of WVU African

American students said they wouldn't have been able to earn their degrees if it weren't for the Marshalls.

The Marshall family grew even larger when Rogers and I conceived our three beautiful children. Gwendolyn, whom we call Gwen, Rogers Jr., and Larry R. were the primary reason Rogers and I worked so hard. And the reason why Rogers always had two or three jobs at a time.

Ironically, when my children were young, I worked at West Virginia University as a part-time cook for the president's house. The other part-time cook there was Evelyn Paige. At that time, the president was Dr. Elvis Stahr, and he was phenomenal. The admiration he showed toward people was inconceivable, and so many people commended him for his generosity. Yet eventually, he proceeded to be the secretary of the army in the Kennedy administration. I was fortunate to be the one who answered the phone when President Kennedy called for Dr. Stahr to finalize his transfer. That was an unforgettable moment. Dr. Elvis Stahr was later succeeded as president by Dr. Paul Miller.

It was an honor to work for the president's house; it was a great opportunity and allowed me to meet a lot of exceptional people. I had worked there for about two years when my neighbor Mary Moore mentioned something to me about putting in an application at Sterling Faucet Company. At first, I was hesitant. Then I thought, *What do I have to lose?*

So Mary and I put in applications at Sterling Faucet Company. Two weeks later, the company called me for an interview. And shortly afterward, I was offered the job of machine operator. I started on the afternoon shift the Friday before Easter, but Good Friday was not a holiday until the following year. Even though I worked all shifts, I always felt bad that Mary didn't get the job. She wasn't hired until a couple of years later.

Before starting at Sterling Faucet Company, I notified President Paul Miller at WVU of my new position. He was very happy and wished me well. It was a bittersweet moment for me to leave the president's house, but I couldn't miss the opportunity to work at Sterling Faucet Company.

It was 1963 when I became the first African American woman to be hired at Sterling Faucet Company. There were about 1,200 people in the union, and only about ten were African American men. Yet the company had been in the Sabraton area in Morgantown since 1940.

Also, at the time I was hired, the civil rights movement was occurring in Morgantown. And I was actively involved in that movement, which opposed racial segregation and discrimination against African Americans. Concurrently, I was a member of the NAACP and the Democratic Women's Club, and I was an active participant in those organizations as well. The Democratic Women's Club was where I began to engage a little in politics, and that was where I first met John "Jay" Rockefeller. Astoundingly, I still have notes from him today.

Soon after I started at Sterling Faucet Company, Marcus Cranford, a distant relative, went to the bowling alley and asked the owner, "Why aren't African Americans allowed to bowl here?"

The owner replied, "I don't have a problem with African Americans bowling here."

When my friend Claudia Woods heard the great news, she called me and said, "We are allowed to bowl."

I exclaimed, "Yes, we are!" We were ecstatic. So that Sunday evening, we started to bowl. At that time, the bowling alley was located at the bottom of the hill of South University Avenue, now named Don Knotts Boulevard.

Additionally, when I passed my sixty-day probation period at Sterling Faucet Company, I joined the United Steelworkers of America union.

Then, several years later, I was elected as the union's recording secretary. I recorded the minutes of the meetings that were held once a month.

United Steelworkers of America was a part of the American Federation of Labor and Congress of Industrial Organizations (known as the AFL-CIO), and Miles Stanley was the first president of the West Virginia Labor Federation AFL-CIO. It was the congress of all unions coming together, inclusive of industrial workers from glass companies, Sterling Faucet Company, and miners.

I became the delegate from the United Steelworkers of America union for the Monongalia-Preston Labor Council, AFL-CIO. This organization consists of representatives from different unions in Monongalia and Preston County. I was elected as their recording secretary as well. We met once a month to discuss issues occurring in our counties and worked together for the same interests. We were also very much involved in politics and came together to elect certain officials into office.

As the delegate from the USWA union for the Monongalia-Preston Labor Council, AFL-CIO, I would go to the courthouse and make sure all the AFL-CIO union members were registered to vote. There would be hundreds of registration cards from unions in Monongalia and Preston Counties. I met a lot of people along the way from working on their cards.

As I was engaged in these organizations, I was beginning to get heavily involved in bowling. My friend Claudia Woods, who had called me saying African Americans were allowed to bowl, suggested that we put together a bowling team and join a league. I agreed. I was always keen to join something new. Claudia and I assembled a few of our friends to have a total of five women on our team. Now we were ready to join a league, and when we joined a league, we would become a part of the Women's International Bowling Congress, known as the WIBC. Wherefore, when Claudia heard from a person at the bowling alley that the Friday Night Women's League had an opening, we immediately joined. We couldn't wait to bowl in the league.

By the time we started to bowl in the league, the Suburban Bowling Lanes had been rebuilt on Chestnut Ridge Road, where they still are. When we went bowling Friday night, we heard another team had dropped out of the league. White teams were dropping out of the league because they heard a Black team was joining the league. That didn't bother us, though. We gathered a few more friends and put together another team. Now we had two teams in the league!

I was still working at Sterling Faucet Company, where I eventually became the store operator. Needless to say, I really enjoyed that. I enjoyed doing inventory and being accountable for all the supplies. I was also responsible for purchasing them. Therefore, I had to be knowledgeable about how much money was allotted for the supplies.

For example, bowling: I attended bowling meetings to be made aware of where my money was being allocated and to know the rules. At one meeting, we were informed that the president of the Morgantown Women's Bowling Association had resigned. Consequently, the vice president at the time moved up to be the president, and I was voted to be the vice president.

Later that day, the president of the Morgantown Women's Bowling Association called me and disclosed that she didn't want to be the president. She asked me, "If I resign as president and you move up to be the president, will you appoint me as the vice president?"

I responded, "Sure." That's when I learned some people want the title but not the job.

Thus, as president of the Morgantown Women's Bowling Association, I started attending state bowling meetings that were held on Sundays.

The first state bowling meeting I was to attend was in Charleston, West Virginia. I had no idea how I was going to get there. We had only one car, and I knew I couldn't take that. Also, I wasn't too familiar with driving on the interstate, which wasn't complete. But I was determined to get to that meeting. I wasn't going to miss that meeting. One of the ladies from bowling called me and said, "Charlene, we were just discussing something. If you can't go to the meeting in Charleston, we have somebody that would take your place." I responded, "OK, I'll let you know." When I hung up that phone, I thought, *I will be there, even if I have to walk.* I was astounded that they had already declared I wasn't going to make it.

Unbeknownst to them, the Marshalls were providing room and board to this young lady who was getting her master's at WVU. She was from Charleston and went home every weekend. So I asked her whether I could ride home with her that weekend. She exclaimed, "Yes!" We arrived in Charleston on Friday night. You couldn't imagine the shocked looks on some of their faces when I walked into that state meeting on Sunday.

The meeting was at a beautiful hotel in Charleston. There were about one hundred women in attendance. However, none of them looked like me. I looked around and thought, *Where are all the Black women?* Then the board of directors came in, and I still couldn't understand why there were no Black women in attendance. And I wanted to know why.

Additionally, as the rules were being discussed, I found out that you had to attend three state meetings before you were qualified to go on the state board. I thought, *I'll do that.* So the following year, my friend Claudia Woods went with me to the state bowling meeting. I told her that next year would be my third year and that I was filling out my papers to get on that board. The next year, I did just that! Claudia nominated me, and I was elected to the West Virginia Women's Board of Directors. I sat on that board for about twelve years.

That board consists of directors and state officers. While on the board, I found out from Martha, the sergeant at arms on the board, that I was the first African American woman to attend a state meeting. That answered my question about why there were no African American women in the meetings. Wherefore, I was always gone. I traveled all over the United States for bowling as national bowling meetings consist of women from all over the world. The meetings have to be held in coliseums because there are so many women in attendance. They are very formal events. They have their own attorneys, and they are very strict with the parliamentary procedures; it is like being in Congress.

In the early 1970s, I attended my first national meeting in Las Vegas. That was also my first airplane ride. I was accompanied by another African American woman from Morgantown who was also going to the meeting. Even still, I was so anxious to get to Las Vegas that I could hardly sit still on the plane. My first time in Las Vegas was exhilarating. I had so much fun that I couldn't wait to go back.

Our 1976 WIBC Women's National Bowling Red, White, and Blue Bicentennial Tournament was held in Denver, Colorado. The board was in attendance for our annual conference meeting, and Ernestine Dutchess, a state officer on the board of directors, was elected to carry the West Virginia flag in the parade of flags. That was the prelude to the tournament, and each person carrying a flag lined up according to when their state had been admitted into the union.

However, before Ernestine Dutchess was elected, she asked me to run against her. I told her no. I said, "You are my friend. I don't want people to think I'm trying to defeat you."

She exclaimed, "Just listen to me! Run against me." Hesitantly, I did, and I was nominated for runner-up.

Ernestine was always very kind to me. She would pick me up and take me to wherever our meetings were held because she knew Rogers and I had only one car. Thus, before the tournament, she called me and said, "I'm not going to the tournament. Therefore, you, as the runner-up, would have to carry the West Virginia flag in the parade of flags." I smiled and said, "You knew the whole time you weren't going." She just laughed.

So when I came out thirty-fifth carrying the West Virginia flag, the crowd was pleased to see me. I was the only African American woman carrying a flag. Wherefore it was an electrifying experience. I really enjoyed it. Afterward, I received a lot of compliments from patrons in the audience.

Meanwhile, I was still bowling in the league and later I received an award for bowling for twenty-five consecutive years in the national tournament. My favorite place to bowl was in Morgantown, West Virginia. I bowled my highest of 265 at Suburban Bowling Lanes. On the contrary, my least favorite place to bowl was in Bismarck, North Dakota, because it was too cold there. I love to travel. As I stated before, seeing new places is fun.

Speaking of traveling to new places, the president of the West Virginia Women's Bowling Association lived in Huntington, West Virginia, and she was relocating to another state with her employer. So, the vice president moved up to be the president. And that president and I spoke frequently because she knew my family very well.

One day she called me and said, "I want to ask you something, but I want to speak to Rogers too." She asked me to bring Rogers to our bowling tournament in Fairmont, West Virginia. When Rogers and I arrived in Fairmont, the president told Rogers, "I want to appoint your wife as vice president of the West Virginia Women's Bowling Association. But that means when the tournament comes up, she's going to have to travel every week. Is that OK with you?"

He responded, "Yes." That was what I was expecting him to say because if he hadn't, I probably would've kicked him under the table and shouted, "You have to say yes!" That was an exceptional opportunity. I became vice president of the West Virginia Women's Bowling Association.

Now I was a state officer on the West Virginia Women's Board of Directors. However, not all the ladies on the board were pleased with my promotion, especially one. She disliked me from the day I walked into the state meeting. When I enter a room, I can always tell who doesn't like me. Every time she saw me talking to someone, she would say, "She's over there campaigning." In contrast, I was simply being myself and not campaigning.

Some of the women demonstrated they were uncomfortable around me through their stares, body language, and not conversing. Still, I proceeded as though their frostiness didn't bother me. Yet behind closed doors, it did. But I wasn't going to let them know that.

THREE
POLITICAL AWARENESS

Although it was a difficult decision, after about fifteen years, I resigned from Sterling Faucet Company. I missed Sterling Faucet Company. I missed being a part of the unions and attending and participating in the monthly meetings. Likewise, Sterling Faucet Company union meetings and bowling national meetings taught me a lot about politics. Our national bowling meetings always had numerous attorneys in attendance. Their presence was imperative in case there were any amendments.

I left Sterling Faucet Company for a job as an inspector for the weights and measures office of the West Virginia Division of Labor. As such, I inspected anything that was sold by weights and measures, mainly gas, dairy products, and meats. And during the inspections, I ensured that the companies were adhering to regulations and agreements pertaining to weights and measures. If they were not, then they were in violation. That's why I sometimes even had to shut down a pump at a gas station if it was not in compliance. Moreover, gas pumps are calibrated to make sure they are giving out the correct amount to customers. Therefore, all compliance issues and violations are documented with the objective that they will be rectified.

Furthermore, I inspected for two long years. I didn't really care for inspecting much, since it is not the type of work I desire to do. Even still, I was very proficient at it. I did not allow my dissatisfaction with the job to affect my performance.

Unfortunately, my father-in-law, Mr. Marshall, became ill during this time; he was diagnosed with Alzheimer's disease. So I stopped working to take care of him. It was a stressful time. Caring for a loved one suffering from Alzheimer's is very strenuous. It is tiring, and it is a thankless job. No one knows all the work you do behind closed doors. Rogers also cared for his father during his illness. But sadly, despite all our efforts, Mr. Marshall passed away in the final stages of the disease. Rogers and I were heartbroken. Yet we persevered through this horrible situation.

After Mr. Marshall's homegoing, I remained at home, taking care of Rogers and our children. At the time, I really didn't have to work. As usual, Rogers was working two or three jobs, while I was busy working around the house. Rogers loved it! He loved how easily accessible I was for him and our children whenever they needed something. One day, he asserted, "You should continue to stay at home, taking care of the children and me." I smiled. I thought, *I could get used to this.* I was enjoying my leisure time. It was rejuvenating, especially since I had been working since, I was twelve.

I started to travel a little bit, visiting family and friends. I visited my sisters in Ohio and New Jersey. Per the normal practice, I went to the Amish market in New Jersey and brought back some spices and meats. Traveling and spending quality time with my family and friends was fun. I loved having the freedom to come and go at will; it felt great not to be on any schedule. I was really considering not working anymore. I knew Rogers and my children were delighted to have me home, and they were appreciative of the quality time we were spending together. At that time, I felt my presence at home was vital, but eventually, *reality* set in. *I am still young,* I thought. *I need to continue to work to receive my social security benefits.*

After about two years of rest and relaxation, I went back to work. It was in 1985 that I started back working at West Virginia University at the information desk. My job was part time, like when I worked for the president's house. Likewise, I was off every summer from May to August. And I was enjoying having my summers off.

I liked that job; I liked interacting with the visitors and employees. Obtaining information for them and assisting them in any way that I could was gratifying for me. I really take pride in helping others.

By this time, some houses in our Greenmont neighborhood were starting to show signs of deterioration. It concerned some of my neighbors and me, so we got together and formed a community group. Then we started to meet at my house. Back then, there was no air-conditioning, so when it was hot, we met outside in my driveway. Our objective was to get the city to take action against a handful of landlords whose dilapidated houses were affecting our entire neighborhood.

At our first meeting, I suggested that we needed a secretary to take the minutes and a spokesperson to oversee the meetings. One person responded, "You're doing all the talking. Why don't you be the spokesperson?"

I laughed, then asked, "Does anyone else have any suggestions?" No one said a word. So I said, "I'll be the spokesperson."

The person who had appointed me to be the spokesperson replied, "OK, you're our president and spokesperson."

I affirmed, "OK." Next, I appointed one of the other ladies to be our secretary.

We began writing letters to every member of the city council, including the city manager and the city clerk. I started going to every city council meeting to see whether I could get some answers to our letters. Still, I went to meeting after meeting, and nothing was done.

I used to attend council meetings occasionally when I was a member of the AFL-CIO. Miles Stanley, president of the West Virginia Labor Federation AFL-CIO, emphasized to his AFL-CIO members that we should always attend council meetings so we could know who our representatives were. I really didn't see the importance of the meetings then, but when some homes in our neighborhood started to deteriorate, I remembered President Miles Stanley's exhortation.

After working a couple of years at the information desk, I started to look for other jobs at WVU. Having summers off was nice, but I began to want a pay increase. Eventually, I received an offer for a full-time job at Student Affairs in the Mountainlair Student Union building, commonly called "the Lair." However, in 2014, WVU president E. Gordon Gee changed the name from Student Affairs to Student Life.

When I worked at Student Affairs, I oversaw student identification and personal rapid transit cards, known as PRT cards. The PRT serves as WVU's primary mass transit system for students, employees, and visitors. My duties included taking students' pictures for their badges and issuing their badges to them. There were no fancy cameras then. So, when the pictures came back, they were on a roll, and I had to separate them out individually.

Nevertheless, I really enjoyed working at Student Affairs. Interacting with the students was fun. I used to tell them when they were misbehaving, "You all better get yourselves together." My daughter Gwen who now works at WVU, but unlike me, she was able to attend and graduate from WVU with a master's degree. Still, back then, when she came to

Political Awareness

visit me at Student Affairs, she would say, "You can't talk to those children like that." And I would exclaim, "Yes, I can! I talk to them like I talk to my own children." Gwen would just look at me and shake her head.

Some of the students I interacted with became good friends of mine. They now have very successful careers and families of their own, including children that are in college. Chip Slaven, a WVU alumnus and my friend, was the interim executive director and CEO of the National School Boards Association. He is now an education leader, equity champion, national speaker, and licensed attorney in Washington, DC. Another good friend of mine and WVU alumnus, David Goldberg, is the president and CEO of Mon Health System. He has a beautiful family and a daughter in college. As a student, David was always coming to my office and using my copy machine, and he was always so nice. Other students couldn't understand why I always allowed him to use my copy machine until I declared, "He is a student too, and he should be able to use my copy machine!" Moreover, Steve Robinson, another WVU alumnus and a good friend, is now Dr. Steve Robinson, who currently resides in Salt Lake City. Jokingly, he used to tell me that David was going to wear out my copy machine, and I would just laugh. Kevin Berry is also a WVU alumnus and my good friend. He was one of the students my daughter told me that I couldn't talk to like that because he was always getting into trouble. I used to tease him and say, "I am going to tell your parents," even though I hadn't met them yet. But later, when I did meet his parents, we became good friends. They are very nice people. Now Kevin Berry is the vice president of alumni relations and CEO of the WVU Alumni Association.

I am extremely honored that I was influential to them when they were getting their education. As I mentioned before, I really take pride in helping others, which is one reason why attending city council meetings was so important to me. It was important for me to help my community with the dilapidated homes in our neighborhood.

I was familiar with who was on the council. So after one city council meeting, I approached the person representing our district to discuss some things that weren't on the agenda, but I was dismissed. Councilor Kenneth Randolph Jr. wouldn't even stop to talk to me. I thought, *How rude!* I wanted to discuss important items about our neighborhood as they were important to me, my family, and my neighbors. And I figured, *We are all working; we are all paying taxes*. A councilor should do what a councilor is elected to do, which is to help people. So I thought, *Someone needs to run against him*.

Now, neighborhood groups were starting to spring up all over Morgantown, and several asked me for help in getting organized and taking their concerns to the city. One group I went down to speak with was in the Marilla area in Morgantown. Ironically, the Marilla neighborhood is located at the bottom of the hill of White Avenue, the street I lived on. Nonetheless, I assisted the residents in starting their association.

An election was coming up, and a rumor started that I would run for the city council. I never found out how that rumor got started, but I had no intention of running for council. I thought, *I'm not going to give anyone a reason to assassinate me*.

Nevertheless, I received several phone calls from people asking me whether I would consider being a candidate for the city council for the Sixth Ward, which was my ward. There are seven wards in Morgantown, and they were recruiting candidates for each ward. Each time they called me, I told them that I was not interested.

Then a lady called me and said they were interviewing candidates for the Sixth Ward at a church and asked me whether I would be interested in going. I answered, "No. I'm just too busy." She said that she was going for the interview, and she was hoping that I would go with her. I responded, "No, not today." She called me back and asked me to go to the interview again. I replied, "No." So she called me a third time and asked me to just ride with her to the interview. I told her, "You have an interview, and I don't. I don't know if they are going to want to interview me."

"Just go. I'll even come to pick you up," she said.

Reluctantly, I went to the interview. At the interview, they asked us several questions about different issues going on around town. Fortunately, I was familiar with most of them, so I was able to elaborate on the topics. Wherefore, when I got home from the interview, one of the interviewers, whom I knew, called me. She said, "We just had a meeting, and we would like for you to be our candidate for the Sixth Ward."

I immediately responded, "No! I just came out. I really wasn't interested."

A couple of nights later, she invited me over to her house. It was only about a ten-minute walk from my house. When I arrived at her house, she asked me, "Why wouldn't you want to be a candidate?" I gave her several reasons why I didn't want to be a candidate. I explained to her that I had never wanted to hold an elected office.

She was an attorney and declared, "If you think there is something that might need legal assistance, or if you have a problem with anything, I will represent you!" I don't know what I was thinking, but *hesitantly*, I agreed to be a candidate. Though ten minutes later, when I got home and took off my coat, I thought, *I must have lost my mind; I'm not doing that.*

Immediately, I called her and exclaimed, "On the way home, I changed my mind!" I'm sure she probably wasn't too happy about that, but we are still good friends. However, I do feel as though I was being recruited.

Over the next few days, four different people called me and told me not to run. This was before the invention of caller ID, so I couldn't see who was calling. And they didn't say who they were, but they all said the same thing: "A Black woman can't win in Morgantown." I thought, *If I can't win, why are you all so worried I'll run?*

Then a semiretired WVU professor who was active in local politics called me, but I didn't have time to speak to him. So, he showed up at my front door. He rang my doorbell and stood on my porch to tell me he was putting together a slate, and my name wasn't on it. He stated, "I have a guy for your ward already, so you should not run." He continued to say that the fathers of the guys on his slate had died in the mines, and the guys had all pulled themselves up by their bootstraps.

My eyebrows raised, and I exclaimed, "Oh really!" His slate consisted of all white men. That's when I invited him into my home. He and I needed to talk. I told him a few stories about people pulling themselves up by their bootstraps and losing fathers to the mines. "Oh, I didn't know that" he replied.

"You didn't ask," I added. After I finished conversing with him, I politely escorted him out of my home. I thought he came there to convince me not to run. That was the deciding factor for me. I figured, *If they are so afraid of me running, then I must have a chance.*

FOUR
MARSHALL'S LAW

After careful consideration, I made a few phone calls and announced to a few people, "I'm running for city council."

Now, there were five of us running for the Sixth Ward, including the incumbent mayor. However, the incumbent mayor was my real opponent. And ironically, the incumbent mayor was Kenneth Randolph Jr. The same person who wouldn't even stop to talk to me after a city council meeting. Who knew two years later I would be running against him?

But there was a group in Morgantown called Cleanup. And a lot of people from WVU were a part of Cleanup. Their focus was cleaning up Morgantown City Hall because we had several landlords who were making their own rules. So, the members of the Cleanup group informed me they would assist me with my campaign, but they would not run it. Therefore, they told me to put together my campaign group and just let them know what I needed.

Samuel Sutton, WVU student body president, whom we called Sam, and some of the other members of the student body board worked with me on my campaign. In addition, my campaign manager was Chip

Slaven. Sam Sutton assembled these students to form my campaign committee.

They would meet at my house, and I would make them pepperoni rolls, as they loved my pepperoni rolls and would always request them. Nonetheless, I told the Cleanup group, "Since I've never been in a campaign before, I would like someone with more knowledge to help me with my slogans and my literature for a handout. And I would like a trifold."

Also, I let them know when my campaign committee would be meeting at my house. Then, members of Cleanup informed me that they had assigned a guy named Bill Case to me, and he would be coming to my house.

I had never met Bill before. But he showed up at my door and rang my doorbell. And when I answered, he asked, "Are you Charlene Marshall?"

I exclaimed, "So you are Bill Case! Come on in."

He talked to me about what he thought I should do for the literature we were going to hand out. Then, he declared, "You have got to tell me some things about yourself and some things you have done!"

I thought, *I haven't done anything yet.*

My mind drew a blank about all the things I'd done, all the committees I'd sat on, and all the positions I'd held. Meanwhile, the students started coming in. Wherefore, Bill said, "I'm going to sit back and listen and take some notes."

The students and I proceeded to come up with our plan for my campaign. Then, after the students left, Bill showed me what he had put together. He had folded a piece of paper into a trifold. And he asked, "What do you think of this?"

He had listed on the trifold these titles: president of the NAACP, officer of the USWA, and officer of the Monongalia-Preston Labor Council, AFL-CIO.

"Where did you get all that from?" I asked.

He said, "To name it all—sometimes it's hard. But as you were talking, I made notes of some of the things you were saying. And these were all the things you had been involved in."

I was impressed. Hence, Bill and I are still good friends today.

Furthermore, I was still working at Student Affairs. So, when my office closed, the students would be right there. They would say, "OK, get your tennis shoes on."

Then, we would go door to door. And Sam Sutton had a speech he would give: "I'm Samuel Sutton, and this is Charlene Marshall. She is running for city council."

Though many residents were impressed with Sam's introduction speech, I still sometimes went door to door by myself. Still, most of the time, the students went with me. Those students were so dedicated to my campaign that I couldn't thank them enough. In addition, we ran my campaign with zero dollars. When my treasurer, Leontyne Clay, would show me my financial report, it would always be all zeros, which was astonishing.

Moreover, sometimes my sons in Ohio and California would call me and ask, "Mom, what are you into now?"

And I would just laugh. Because they knew I was always doing something. It was almost as if our roles had reversed. Even so, one time, my son Larry R. in Ohio called me and asked what I was into now.

I replied, "I'm running for city council. And my real opponent is the incumbent mayor."

There was complete silence. Then, he exclaimed, "Oh, Mom, he's the mayor! He knows everybody!"

I'm not sure whether that was what I was expecting my son to say, but that was his honest answer. So, I asserted, "I'm not *worried* about him knowing everybody. I'm concerned with making a change to the city council and dismissing these landlords or 'slumlords' who are making their own rules."

These landlords had several students in one building and provided them with only one parking space. Thereby leaving the rest of the students to park on the street and inevitably causing the streets to become crowded. As a result, other vehicles were unable to get through.

Meantime, the Cleanup group had sent in money for six of the candidates in six of the wards. Afterward, each candidate was asked to write a statement about what we wanted to see done in Morgantown. We were going to get the statements published in a newspaper. But we didn't think we could get good publicity from our local newspaper. The reason was that the incumbent mayor and the newspaper editor were good friends—although now our local newspaper is more effective. Nevertheless, there was an attorney there who had a relative with a newspaper company in another city in West Virginia. We believed we could get a better deal and better publicity with that newspaper. So we sent our statements to that newspaper company.

When the newspaper came out, it was about the size of an *Esquire* magazine. Each candidate had a page. And we had thousands of copies that we had to deliver. At the time, I had a Nissan Maxima with a sunroof. Some people from the Cleanup group, other volunteers, and another candidate packed the back of my car with the newspapers. One of the volunteers sat in the back and folded the newspapers while I drove. Then she handed the folded newspapers to the other candidate while he stood up and tossed them out of my sunroof. The volunteer was so tiny that she could squeeze into the back seat corner with all those newspapers. And when the candidate tossed the newspapers out of my sunroof into the yards, he would scream, *"Paperboy!"*

We delivered those newspapers until six in the morning. We were determined to cover the area that was assigned to us. Cleanup members had cut up a map of Morgantown into equal squares and numbered the squares. They gave each candidate a square containing the areas where the candidate needed to deliver the newspapers. We had to shade in the areas on the square when we delivered the newspapers to them. Afterward, there was a picnic where we met back up with our shaded squares. At the picnic, we put our numbered squares back together and pieced together the map of Morgantown. We showed that the entire city of Morgantown had been covered.

In addition, Cleanup members held a press conference for the six candidates they had sponsored. Not all six were present. I was there with my good friend Priscilla Blue. They were taking photos of the candidates. Also, a reporter from the radio station showed up with his tape recorder and began to interview the candidates. He had his microphone and started asking them questions. He interviewed a few candidates and then started to pack up his tape recorder. Ms. Blue asked him, "Are you leaving?"

He exclaimed, "Yes!"

Ms. Blue stated, "Well, Mrs. Marshall is a council candidate, and you didn't interview her."

He exclaimed, "I ran out of tape!" My friend and I knew that wasn't true. What good reporter runs out of tape on only four people?

I thought, *The election hasn't even started yet, and I'm already getting shunned. I might as well get my thick skin on because I can see what's going to happen. They don't think there's even a need to talk to me because they don't think I'm going to be elected.*

So I just tried to get my guard up.

Nonetheless, the League of Women Voters always had a session before the election to allow the citizens an opportunity to interview and speak with the candidates. The session was held at Suncrest United Methodist Church. All the candidates were lined up around a table in order of their wards. There are seven wards. And several candidates were running for each ward.

So, there was a total of about sixteen candidates. We each had a chance to introduce ourselves and had a few minutes to say something. Then, we would pass the microphone down to the next candidate. Ironically, the same reporter from the radio station who didn't interview me at the press conference was at Suncrest United Methodist Church. He was there recording because the next morning, he was going to appear on a talk show. He was going to be making comments about each candidate and also airing a few minutes of what each candidate had to say.

I was so excited when I went to work at Student Affairs the next morning. I couldn't wait to listen to the talk show on the radio. When the talk show came on, the reporter started with the first ward candidates. He continued to go down the line. As he went down the line, I could picture each candidate at the table. When he started to speak about this one candidate, I thought, *OK, I'm next. Let me see what he says about me.*

Then, he *skipped* me.

He went to the next person. I was in my office, screaming at the radio, "I was next! I was next!"

I jumped up and went to the phone. But before I could get the number and dial it, several Caucasian women from the League of Women

Voters had already called into the show. He told them he had to go to break and that was why he skipped me. However, I wasn't going to let this incident slide as I had at the press conference. So when I got him on the phone, I told him, "I know what you did."

He asked me, "Do you want to say a few words now?" I said a few words. Yet I was so upset that I didn't articulate my words as I would have liked to. Therefore, I knew early on that it wasn't going to be easy.

Unfortunately, I encountered more situations like that, but I never wavered. I knew some people thought I wasn't qualified to run and wanted me to stay in my place. But no one that has ever changed the world has stayed in his or her place. And I wasn't going to either! My place is wherever people are. I enjoy helping people. Consequently, I will do what it takes to accomplish that.

Even still, I had great support. One of the ladies from the League of Women Voters who beat me to the phone to call into the talk show spoke with me frequently. She heard from someone that I had changed my mind about running. You have to get so many signatures from registered voters in your area to have your name on the ballot. And I wasn't getting my signatures. So while she was pregnant, she went out in the rain and snow and started getting the signatures I needed. She wanted to make sure I wouldn't back down. Then, I continued to get my signatures. Even now, when I see her son, whom she was carrying at the time, I tell him that story. I know I must've told him that story numerous times. Even when she saw me, she would ask me whether I remembered when she was pregnant and went out in the rain and snow getting signatures. I would exclaim, "How can I not remember that? You were helping me so I wouldn't change my mind!"

This was a huge election. Everyone was watching. The current city council members had been in those positions for years, including the incumbent mayor. He had been in his position for five years. People were looking for a change. The night of the election at city hall was so electrifying as the returns were coming in. I swear some of my opponents paced back and forth about fifty times. Some of them were so anxious. Surprisingly, I was nice and calm.

So, in April of 1991, I was elected to Morgantown City Council for the Sixth Ward. I defeated my four opponents, including the incumbent mayor, by a landslide. It was a great feeling considering that I had no intention of running. I often say I didn't have a plan, but somebody had a plan for me. And that plan helped me to move forward. Everything I learned during my journey prepared me for my destination!

FIVE
ELECTED OFFICIAL

SHORTLY AFTER I WAS elected to council, my uncle was fishing in the Monongahela River, and he didn't come home late at night. His family went to look for him and found out he had had a heart attack and had fallen into the river. His funeral was the same week as the state bowling meeting. That was going to be the only meeting I had missed in years. But I knew that when I missed that meeting there would be people, especially one person, campaigning for a new vice president. That one person was the one who had disliked me from the day I walked into the state meeting.

So I told the ladies in Morgantown that I wasn't going to be able to attend the state bowling meeting because my uncle's funeral was coming up. I said, "But if I get defeated for vice president, just nominate me for a seat on the board."

They shouted, "That's going backward!"

I responded, "To me, it's not. It's me staying on that board and nobody being able to tell me when to get off. I'll decide that for myself." I always thought that at some point, you take control of your own life and don't let anyone push you around.

Thus, in May of 1991, I attended my uncle's funeral. In addition, I became a board member on the West Virginia Women's Board of Directors again. However, I never attended another meeting. Yet they couldn't fill my position until my term was up. Meanwhile, the new city council members were going to be meeting for the first time to elect the mayor of Morgantown. They always met on the first Tuesday in July. I knew it wasn't going to be an easy decision. But I was accustomed to things not being easy.

They met on July 2, 1991. On the night of the election, the council chamber was packed. People were standing along the walls, sitting on the floors, and squeezing into the hallways and stairwells. However, my husband didn't go to city hall that night. But later, he told me that his cousin's son was there—yet city hall was so packed that he had to stand in the doorway because he couldn't get in. But when it was announced that I was elected mayor, he ran out and ran back to our street and shouted, "Charlene's the mayor! Charlene's the mayor!"

On July 2, 1991, I was elected the mayor of Morgantown. I was elected on the first night, even though it took several ballots. Afterward, when I went to the mayor's desk, I was a nervous wreck. We took a recess because the news wanted to go on air right away. It was a huge election, and everyone was watching. One of the television stations from Clarksburg had a van set up and was ready to go live. So the news reporter started to interview me. And one of his first questions was "What are you going to do as mayor because you are a university person?"

I declared, "You can stop right there! I am not a university person. I work at the university. I am a Morgantown resident, and we should all work together and try to get along." I added, "I live in Morgantown, but I was born and raised in Osage."

I wanted to make sure I cleared that up just in case people thought that I didn't want anyone to know I was from Osage. I figured, *I'll take care of that right away.*

After the interview, we went back inside to resume our meeting. I was so nervous. I really wanted to say, "*Why don't we all go home and reconvene next week?*" But I didn't because I knew there was business to take care of. When the meeting was adjourned, everyone came up to me and congratulated me. I was so overwhelmed. I couldn't wait to get home.

The next day, when I went to work, someone came to my office window. It was a reporter from the *Charleston Gazette*. The *Charleston Gazette* had sent a reporter and photographer to talk to me and take photos of me. I wondered, *How am I going to ask to be excused from work?*

So I just left. We went all through the town. They interviewed me and took photos of me. And I was thinking, *What is the big deal?*

Then, Uniontown's newspaper reporters made an appointment to come up and interview me and take photos of me. They took photos of me at WVU, in the back of the Mountainlair Student Union building. They wrote over a half page about me and listed some of the activities I had done. And I was still thinking, *What is the big deal?* However, our local newspaper didn't announce that I was mayor until a couple of days after the election.

Yet on July 3rd, I was still wrapping my head around being elected mayor of Morgantown. Then, I received a call saying that I was scheduled to be in the Fourth of July parade. Immediately, I had to prepare for that.

On the Fourth of July, they sent a car to come to get me. The chief of police was riding with me. It was an extraordinary experience riding in the Fourth of July parade. People were screaming as we rode by. Mothers brought their daughters out to show them a woman could be mayor. The mothers were pointing and waving and showing me to their daughters. As we rode by the Citizens Bank of Morgantown, someone from the crowd yelled, "Motor Mouth!"

I tried to sit still like I had good sense. But eventually, I yelled back, "Motor Mouth!"

The chief of police began to laugh. He asked, "Is this parade for the Fourth of July or just for you? Because you know everybody on the street."

I laughed and said, "That is my good friend from bowling. We play on the same Friday Night Women's League. We nicknamed each other Motor Mouth because both of us can get a little loquacious sometimes."

The entire parade experience was unimaginable. I was introduced as mayor to the city of Morgantown by Michael Oliverio Sr. He was the first person to announce me as mayor to the city of Morgantown.

Nevertheless, after the parade, I told my daughter Gwen that my good friend from bowling was at the parade and that she yelled out "Motor Mouth!"

I told her that I yelled it back. Gwen sighed and said, "Oh, Mom, surely you didn't do that!"

I answered, "Yes, I did. That is my friend. I'm not going to change how I speak to my friend." As usual, Gwen just looked at me and shook her head. That became my friend's and my normal routine. For each parade I was in, she would be standing in different spots. I wouldn't know where until she yelled out "Motor Mouth!" And then I would yell it back.

When I was elected mayor, I became too busy to remain a member of the West Virginia Women's Board of Directors and president of the NAACP. It was funny—when I was elected to the city council and still working at Student Affairs, WVU student Steve Robinson declared I was running the NAACP, my church (St. Paul AME) and the city council out of the Student Affairs Office. Also, after I was elected mayor, I encountered the gentleman that had come to my house to say I wasn't on his slate several more times.

One day, he came to Student Affairs and saw me talking to the maintenance people. He asked, "When are you going to change? You talk to everybody."

"I'm not!" I exclaimed. I thought, *Because I'm the mayor now, I am not supposed to talk to certain people? That's not going to happen.*

He continued, "You really don't know what you did."

"Excuse me?" I said.

He added, "No one has ever beat a Randolph."

I smiled and said, "Well, I'm glad I am the first." I knew my former opponent Kenneth Randolph Jr. had an uncle in politics, Senator Jennings Randolph. He was a well-known politician in Morgantown. He was most notable for his service in the US House of Representatives and the US Senate. He even has a bridge named after him. The Jennings Randolph Bridge was built in 1977. It is the largest Pratt truss bridge in North America. It crosses the Ohio River between Chester, West Virginia, and East Liverpool, Ohio. But obviously, I didn't let that stop me.

However, that wasn't my biggest first. Unbeknownst to me and everyone else, *I made history* when I was elected the mayor of Morgantown on July 2, 1991. A few months after I was elected mayor, my good friend Carolyn Bailey Lewis was researching records and could not find any other city in the state that had elected a Black woman as mayor. Wherefore, I became the first African American woman mayor in West Virginia. Now I think, *It was 1991. You'd think there would have been others before me.*

Nonetheless, my good friend Carolyn Bailey Lewis—now an author, and Dr. Carolyn Bailey Lewis—and I met at St. Paul AME Church. She spent much of her career at WNPB-TV in Morgantown and was named director and general manager in 1993. That made her the first African American woman to manage a full-service public television station in the United States. And her good friend Fred Rogers from the children's television series *Mister Rogers' Neighborhood* was there to honor her. Furthermore, I will always be grateful for my friend researching that information.

But five weeks after the new city council was elected, the city manager resigned. So as mayor, first on my agenda was electing my city manager. We did a nationwide search and had over 130 applicants. After the process of elimination, we elected Dan Boroff, who I thought was the greatest city manager *ever*. His humble personality, easy accessibility, and input on many projects distinguished him from any other candidate. He was in Clarksburg. So the people on the city council in Clarksburg would always tease me and say I stole their city manager.

Dan and I had a great partnership. Dan and I both believe teamwork is the key to success. You have to work together. There's nothing you can't achieve when you work together—because behind every great mayor is a great city manager! I often tell people, whatever you're doing, and especially with some of the things I've had the opportunity to do, you don't do it alone. You're standing on someone's shoulders, and there are a lot of people there who are willing to help you. Dan and I went on to do some fantastic things in Morgantown. Still, I believe the new city council and Dan Boroff are the ones who turned this city around. When they arrived, we started to see a lot of improvements.

Although *some things* didn't change. The photographer for our local newspaper would come to different events I attended and take pictures of everyone. Then, when the newspaper came out, you wouldn't see me in any of the photos. One Saturday, I went to University High School for a forum about smoking. When the newspaper came out the next day, I wasn't included in the photo. I knew when that flash went off I wasn't in that picture! That Sunday morning, my friend called me and asked, "Why didn't you go to University High yesterday?"

I asked, "What makes you think I didn't go?"

She responded, "Your picture isn't in the newspaper."

I exclaimed, "I didn't expect it to be!"

I added, "You see that black hand lying on the table? That's me." Only part of my hand was in the photo. Several people called the newspaper and complained. I came to find out that the photographer had taken two pictures. The other picture I was in…they didn't publish that one.

In another incident, I was at an event in Blacksville, West Virginia. The next day, I asked one of the guys who was at the event, "Did you see my picture in the newspaper?"

He said, "I saw your foot." That time, we were sitting outside, and my foot was pointing out from underneath the table. However, by then, I had developed a pretty thick skin, and I didn't allow it to bother me. I had to stay focused on the task at hand. And that was to make Morgantown an inviting city that people wanted to come to and visit. That's why in many ways, politics is a lot like bowling. Both are a matter of setting things up and knocking them down, be they pins or the correction of social problems. You have to handle it one issue at a time.

SIX
REBIRTH AND REGROWTH

WE WANTED TO BRING growth to Morgantown. That was our primary goal. Also, a lot of areas needed to be revitalized. Many citizens complained about landlords having too many people in one house and their cars crowding the streets, thus leaving no room for other cars to get through the streets. In addition, city employees hadn't had a raise in years, and we wanted to rectify that. Thus, we made some major improvements. The police department and fire department received new vehicles. City employees were given raises. Things were starting to turn around.

Additionally, Governor Caperton came to visit Morgantown. This was when we were first looking into the development of the waterfront. Mrs. Ruby, the wife of the late J. W. Ruby, whom Ruby Memorial Hospital in Morgantown is named after, was present as well. Yet Florence Merow, a former state delegate and former Morgantown mayor, was the one who initially had the idea of developing the waterfront.

At the time, the waterfront was a dump. So, we began implementing our plans for the waterfront project. We developed the Caperton Trail, named after the governor. It is located at the heart of the trail system, spanning the north-south length of Morgantown and Star City. The rail-trail is six miles of paved surface, perfect for rollerblading, walking, and biking. It is an urban trail with easy access to neighboring restaurants and shopping areas that cater to the trail users in Morgantown and Star City. It was the perfect time to develop the rail-trail. People were really starting to get interested in going outdoors and exercising. It was a complement to the area. The Caperton Trail has been commended in numerous articles emphasizing what we have to offer in Morgantown.

But it took teamwork to clean up the waterfront. Periodically Morgantown had cleanup days where we went around the city with trash bags picking up garbage. And the waterfront was one of the places we went. As mayor, I participated in those cleanup days. Hence, a lot of people's first encounter with me was when I was picking up garbage. They were astonished by me being the mayor and picking up trash. I asked them this: if I couldn't pick up trash as mayor, how could I expect anyone else to? It started with me! Today, when I see some of those people, they tell me that they still remember that.

Also, we acquired the property that we built the Morgantown Marriott at Waterfront Place on. It overlooks the Monongahela River. But securing that property wasn't as easy as some people may think. It was quite a negotiation. For instance, the US Postal Service wanted to put one of its distribution centers there. The postmaster at the time arranged a meeting with the city to discuss the distribution center. And I went to Dan Boroff and told him this was a meeting he must attend. So the postmaster and another gentleman met with us at city hall. They told us they were going to put their distribution center there. Dan Boroff said, "We were hoping to put something there that would have a continual revenue flow coming in. We could assist you in finding another location."

Yet the postmaster was adamant about having the distribution center there. After the meeting, Dan said, "Mayor, we've got to do something. I think we can make some other arrangements."

So he and I wrote letters to Senator John "Jay" Rockefeller, Senator Robert Byrd, and another congressman asking them to step in and not allow the US Postal Service to put a distribution center there. After several weeks and Senator Robert Byrd getting involved, we received a phone call saying the US Postal Service distribution center wouldn't go there.

Then, others had the next rights to the property. One company was the Kroger Company out of Cincinnati, Ohio. It tried to obtain the property. One day at home, I received a phone call from the Kroger headquarters. The person I spoke with said that Morgantown had been good to Kroger. The company had two stores there and was looking to put up a third. Still, the person informed me that if the property would serve Morgantown better, the company would relinquish its rights to the property. So it did. And those were some of the challenges we faced while obtaining that property.

Besides that, we implemented a smoking ban in restaurants and created designated smoking areas. In addition, we required helmets for cyclists. Those were some of the health issues we wanted to work on. Morgantown already had a helmet requirement for motorcyclists. But doctors were saying they were having more patients come in with bicycle injuries. At the time, people thought we were crazy for focusing on eliminating smoking in restaurants and requiring cyclists to wear helmets. However, now you can see those are laws and requirements in most states.

Still, I stayed focused on keeping restaurants, theatres, and hotels integrated in Morgantown. As an activist, long before I was elected to the city council, I was instrumental in integrating Morgantown's restaurants, theatres, and hotels. During that time, Hotel Morgan, located in downtown Morgantown, didn't serve African Americans. Also, there were few places for African Americans to eat then. Therefore, some professors from WVU were involved in breaking down discrimination in restaurants, theatres, and hotels as well. One restaurant, in particular, was the Flame. It was located in downtown Morgantown. It was owned by a family who had decided to turn their home into a steak house.

It was a very popular eatery in Morgantown. Thus, membership was required for people to go to this restaurant, although the members didn't have any paperwork to show they were members. One day, two Caucasian female professors from WVU invited Rogers and me to the Flame. They were "members." So, when we arrived at the restaurant, one of the waiters came to the door and asked, "May I help you?"

The two professors said, "Yes. We are members, and we have reservations for dinner."

Then, immediately, the waiter said, "Wait, I have to get someone."

And as expected, she went back and got the owner. The owner came to the door and asked us again, "May I help you?"

Again, the two professors replied, "We have dinner reservations; we've been here before." However, the entire time the owner was looking at Rogers and me. So he fumbled around, looking to see where he was going to seat us. Meanwhile, we were standing outside in the cold. And it wasn't crowded in there at all that night.

Nonetheless, eventually, they seated us upstairs where *no one* else was seated. It was an eerie feeling. But still, we had dinner. As we were leaving the restaurant, I made a special effort to find the owner and tell him that we had enjoyed the dinner. I also asked whether Rogers and I could have memberships because we would like to come back sometime.

The owner immediately said, "The memberships are all filled up right now. But when we have openings, I will let you know." Yet he never asked me for any contact information.

Furthermore, two professors from WVU, Drs. Virgil and Sophia Peterson, would frequent restaurants with diverse groups of students. That was the reward they gave their students for their accomplishments. However, some restaurants wouldn't allow them in when they had African American students with them. Nonetheless, Drs. Virgil and Sophia Peterson continued to take diverse groups of their students to restaurants with the anticipation of breaking down discrimination barriers.

In fact, Mr. and Mrs. Peterson went to the Flame that same night after we had left. And they didn't have memberships. They said they got in, and no one asked them for proof of membership. Instead, they said they asked the Flame for memberships, and the Flame gave *them* memberships. But as usual, there was no paperwork to show for it.

When they left, they immediately called me and told me what had happened. Then, we all met up at a friend's house. I immediately filled out the paperwork to file a complaint with the West Virginia Human Rights Commission. Hence, we sent out my paperwork that same night. I was not going to let them get away with that. And how naive of them to think that they were going to. Yet I didn't want financial compensation. I just wanted them to know that we were aware of what they had done and to remedy it!

Additionally, in 1992, I received the Martin Luther King Jr. Achievement Award from West Virginia University. It was the university's second year giving out that award. I was honored! However, of course, not everyone was happy for me. I heard from a friend that some Blacks asked, "Why is she receiving that award? She hasn't done anything for Black people."

Unbeknownst to them, the award honors the person who best exemplifies working to fulfill King's commitment. The person who has made a substantial contribution toward advancing causes important to humanity, such as civil rights, human rights, humanitarianism, social action and advocacy, and equality. A lot of people viewed me as instrumental in the community. Yet I still received criticism from some African Americans. But I didn't waver. I've learned you can't allow anyone to hold you back. If people are not coming along, you just move forward without them.

However, when some people got into trouble, they would name-drop and say, "Call 'the Marshall.' I know the mayor." "The Marshall" was what some people called me when I became the mayor. But I could do only so much. I wasn't going to do anything to get myself removed from office. So I guess some people didn't like my response when they got into trouble.

Even still, in 1994, I was named Mayor of the Year for the state of West Virginia by the West Virginia Municipal League during the league's annual conference. That is a *distinguished* achievement. The city clerk at the time was the one who nominated me for the award. She filled out and submitted the award nomination form. I will always be appreciative of her for that. It shows that hard work doesn't go unnoticed. Because as mayor, regardless of the criticism, you have to be confident in your decision-making and not let others think they can turn you around and make you afraid of whatever your thoughts may be. That has helped me more times than I can remember.

Also, around 1994, I participated in the efforts to renovate and revitalize the historic Metropolitan Theatre, which some people call the Met. It consists of a single-floor auditorium with a balcony and is located in downtown Morgantown. And outside the theatre is a statue of Morgantown native Jesse "Don" Knotts, who frequently performed there.

Furthermore, the theatre was owned by the Comuntzis family, the family of Dorothy Comuntzis, who was Morgantown's first woman mayor. Years later, at a city council meeting during Women's History Month, I was privileged to receive, along with Dorothy Comuntzis—her family receiving hers in her honor—a plaque honoring women mayors of Morgantown. Dorothy Comuntzis's and my plaques were hung in Morgantown City Hall, honoring her as Morgantown's first woman mayor and me as Morgantown's first African American woman mayor.

However, during the time around 1994, Congressman Alan Mollohan and a friend of his wanted to save the Met because they didn't want to see it torn down. In addition, a local jeweler started a campaign to save the Metropolitan. Moreover, a lot of people were interested in saving the Met, so they gave donations. Also, there was a committee to help save the Met, and there were quite a few people on that committee. Thus, after much work, Congressman Alan Mollohan was able to obtain some money to start the purchase of the Metropolitan Theatre. But the money had to be funneled through the city. So my city manager, Dan Boroff, had the check for the funds.

Wherefore, a meeting was scheduled at the historic Metropolitan Theatre to deliver the check to the owner. And I had the check to bring to the meeting. At the meeting, the owner, Mr. Comuntzis; the jeweler who had started the campaign to save the Metropolitan; and I were all on the stage. The theatre had been closed for several years. So they cleared off the stage and put a table and three chairs up there for us.

Meanwhile, as we were sitting there, I thought, *This gives me cold chills. Here I am sitting on the stage, this poor little Black girl from Osage, with a check to begin the purchase of the Metropolitan Theatre. And as a child, I had to sit up in the balcony because African Americans weren't allowed on the first floor.*

Additionally, I was thinking, *You never know what's going to happen in your lifetime.* I would've *never* imagined that in a place where I hadn't been allowed on the first floor, I'd someday be sitting on the stage with a check to help renovate the building.

Nevertheless, I handed the check to the jeweler who had started the campaign to save the Met, and he handed the check to Mr. Comuntzis. Though the committee stood around on stage, no one on that stage knew what I was thinking and what I had experienced there as a child. That's why I tell people to be careful how they treat others because you *never* know if your paths will cross again!

Furthermore, a year prior, the Federal Bureau of Investigation was having a new building built in Clarksburg, West Virginia. Hence, FBI employees from Washington, DC, were coming in by busloads to visit Morgantown and the surrounding areas. And I was told when and where the buses would be coming so I could be there to greet them.

One time, the buses came to West Virginia University. It was great because I was still employed by WVU at Student Affairs. So I was able to give the FBI employees a tour of the campus, which I knew they would enjoy. Then, another time, buses with FBI employees pulled into the Chick-fil-A in Morgantown's University Town Centre. And I was there to introduce myself, talk to them about the area, and take them to the construction site where the new FBI office was being built in Clarksburg, West Virginia. It was a busy time. But we were hoping that the FBI employees from Washington, DC, would be interested in relocating to West Virginia to work at the new FBI office.

In addition, city manager Dan Boroff, other agency employees, and I rented a van to go to Washington, DC, to speak with the FBI employees there. It was a nice overnight trip. We spoke with them at the J. Edgar Hoover Building, the headquarters of the Federal Bureau of Investigation. Additionally, as I was speaking, I said, "It's my birthday! And I'm here spending my sixtieth birthday with you!"

They laughed. They couldn't believe I was sixty.

But we enjoyed speaking with them. We believed the conversation was very productive. In 1995, some FBI employees from Washington, DC, did relocate to West Virginia to work at the new FBI office. Otis Cox, Office of Personnel Management background investigator for the FBI, was one of the first employees who moved to Morgantown. He also attended St. Paul AME Church.

Yet unbeknownst to me, when I attended church one Sunday, Otis Cox was there to present me with the Exceptional Service in the Public Interest Award from the Federal Bureau of Investigation. I was amazed! Everything I had done was because I enjoyed helping others and not because I was expecting any recognition. However, I am still grateful.

Though while I was working at Student Affairs, the students took a survey. And the survey asked them, "What do you like most about being on campus?"

Most of the students answered, "Having the mayor on campus."

I wasn't aware of the survey until WVU's president asked me, "Did you know there was a survey taken?"

I exclaimed, "No!" Then, he proceeded to tell me what the students had said. I was speechless. That was one of the few times I didn't have *anything* to say. How I was feeling was beyond words. I was absolutely astonished!

Moreover, I continued to work at Student Affairs until I retired from WVU in 1997. It was a sad moment. I did not want to depart from the students. But as I mentioned before, most of the students became good friends of mine. So I kept in contact with them.

And after I retired from WVU, my plan was to stay at home. I had been reelected for one more year as mayor, my reelection making me the mayor from 1991 to 1998. My seven terms as mayor set a record in the two-hundred-plus-year history of the city. No one had *ever* been mayor in Morgantown for more than five years.

However, before my year term ended as mayor, some WVU students were telling me I should run for the West Virginia House of Delegates. I thought, *No way!* I was content with my seven terms as mayor.

Nonetheless, in 1998, I was asked to become a candidate for the legislature. I don't know whether I was influenced by the students telling me to run for the West Virginia House of Delegates or by a higher power telling me my journey wasn't over yet; either way, I decided to become a candidate for the legislature. And my good friend Steve Robinson had already graduated from WVU and had moved back to Virginia, where he lived. But when I informed him, I was going to be a candidate for the West Virginia House of Delegates, he came back to Morgantown. He stayed with Rogers and me for two weeks to help me get started with my campaign. And he was extremely helpful. I will always be grateful to him for that.

My first campaign manager was Jeremy Posey, a WVU student. He was phenomenal. He did such an excellent job with my campaign that several people asked me where I got him from.

Campaigning for the West Virginia House of Delegates was different from campaigning for the city council. We needed funds to campaign for the West Virginia House of Delegates. So we had to have fundraisers. Also, we had great contributions. Some people were very generous with sending in money for the election.

After Jeremy Posey's assistance with my campaign concluded, Bob Musick became my second campaign manager. I was introduced to Bob by my daughter Gwen, who met him first. He was one of her instructors at WVU. Thereafter, Bob and his wife, Tanya, became good friends of mine. I depend on them for many things. In addition, I asked Bob to emcee my eightieth birthday party, which was held at the Erickson Alumni Center. He did such an amazing job. And there were so many people in attendance that it was standing room only.

Unbeknownst to me, Bob had told numerous people to come out and celebrate my life! Additionally, when I was the president of the NAACP, Bob served in that organization as well. Moreover, Bob is very outgoing, and he knows a lot of people. He had already been involved in politics before I met him, as he had been campaign chairman for a number of candidates. So I figured, *I will win with him!*

Thus, in May of 1998, I won the nomination for the West Virginia House of Delegates. Surprisingly, I led the ticket. I began to think, *I may win that seat in November for the general election.* Yet I stayed on as mayor until the election in November was over. I didn't want to be too confident that I would win. But I believed several people on Morgantown City Council wanted me to resign so that I wouldn't be a candidate for mayor again. Though unbeknownst to them, I wasn't planning on running for mayor again. Furthermore, in November of 1998, I was elected as a Democrat to the West Virginia House of Delegates to represent the Forty-fourth District. *Then,* I resigned as mayor!

SEVEN
MY JOURNEY

NOVEMBER OF 1998 WAS a momentous time for me. I was featured in the November edition of *Ebony Magazine*. It has Oprah and Danny Glover on the front cover. The article is titled *Women Mayors* and subtitled *Black women mayors*. I was one of the ten African American women mayors *Ebony Magazine* selected to be in this article. I'm not sure how the magazine knew about me. But I was elated when I received the phone call. I sent in my picture, and next to my picture, there is a magnificent article written about me. I *never* dreamed one day I would be featured in *Ebony Magazine*. Yet I tell people that is probably the closest I'll *ever* get to Oprah.

Even still, being elected to the West Virginia House of Delegates and being away from home for extended periods was a new experience. I didn't come home from Charleston every weekend because that would've been a lot of traveling. So sometimes, I would be away from home for a couple of weeks at a time. Therefore, I am appreciative of my family for being so supportive. I could not have succeeded without them.

As a member of the West Virginia House of Delegates, I worked on some bills pertaining to civil rights. One bill, in particular, was the Prohibition of Racial Profiling Bill. This bill stated the following:

The Legislature finds that the use by a law-enforcement officer of race, ethnicity, or national origin in deciding which persons should be subject to traffic stops, stops and frisks, questioning, searches, and seizures is a problematic law-enforcement tactic. The reality or public perception of racial profiling alienates people from the police, hinders community policing efforts, and causes law-enforcement officers and law-enforcement agencies to lose credibility and trust among the people law enforcement is sworn to protect and serve. Therefore, the West Virginia Legislature declares that racial profiling is contrary to public policy and should not be used as a law-enforcement investigative tactic.

At the time, racial profiling was a serious problem, not just in West Virginia but throughout the United States. Thus, I was happy to be involved in implementing that bill.

Also, I enjoyed having the youth from Morgantown come to Charleston and be pages for me. Our page program gave the youth from West Virginia's public and nonpublic schools an opportunity to serve in the West Virginia legislature. The pages served the House of Representatives by assisting members of the House with their legislative duties. Some of the duties included carrying documents, messages, and letters between various congressional offices. Wherefore, the pages served on the chamber floor, made deliveries throughout campus, and supported member offices.

One page I remember is Dominick Claudio. He was about twelve years old. His family lived in the same townhome complex as my daughter, and his mother and my daughter became friends. Therefore, one day, I asked his mother, "Would your boys like to be pages in Charleston?"

She exclaimed, "Sure! That would be great!"

So, Dominick and his older brother became pages. Immediately, I noticed Dominick's enthusiasm for the page program. He was always asking compelling questions that showed his interest in the government and how it worked. And I was privileged to be there to answer his questions. Now, Dominick is a successful businessman and former member of the Star City Council, where he served for ten years.

Many of the youth that served as pages tell me today that they remember that experience and that they are very grateful for the opportunity. In addition, Dominick mentioned he was honored that I asked him and his brother to be pages. He said the page program and my affable personality gave him the confidence he needed to begin his path to success. Furthermore, I am thankful for all my pages and for the vital role I was blessed to play in their lives. Nonetheless, I represented the Forty-fourth District from 1998 to 2002.

Unfortunately, in 2002, the reconstruction of Osage began. The Star City Bridge, also known as the Edith B. Barill Bridge, named after a former mayor of Star City, West Virginia, was reconstructed from a two-lane to a five-lane bridge. It connects Star City, West Virginia, with Interstate 79 and western Monongalia County. Wherefore, the bridge serves as a primary means of access to the north side of Morgantown. As the bridge crosses over the Monongahela River, it extends from Boyers Avenue, which is in Monongalia County, to Osage Road. As a result, many homes in Osage were demolished. Therefore, my mother and several other residents were forced to vacate Osage. So understandably, that was a very sorrowful time for the citizens of Osage and even me because I still consider Osage home.

Nevertheless, in 2004, I was reelected as a Democrat to the West Virginia House of Delegates to represent the Fifty-first District. Again, I led the ticket. Moreover, there were some changes, including changes to all the district numbers. Monongalia County was changed from District Forty-four to District Fifty-one. Even still, we had some great supporters and contributors for this election as well.

Additionally, I served on some outstanding committees. One committee I served on was the Finance Committee. I am told funds I was able to obtain for a couple of projects are still being received today. Also, I was appointed as chaplain. However, I'm not a minister. But I oversaw the lineup at our ceremony, so when the speaker announced the individuals, you knew who was next. The individuals were lined up according to who was going to lead the prayer, who was going to lead the flag salute, or who was going to make additional announcements. And along with the secretary who worked with me, I made sure that if there was something the individual needed to memorize, it was put in the desk drawer for them.

Furthermore, I was the chaplain for about seven years. And I had the opportunity to make contact with people from all across the state. Some of the delegates would tell me if they had someone in their area that they thought would be great to come to the legislature to lead the morning prayer. Because the prayer didn't always have to be led by a delegate. Therefore, one morning, I was privileged to have my pastor, Pastor Cain from Kingdom EMC Church, which I am now attending, come and lead the morning prayer; that was very special for me. It was always very important for me to have someone from Morgantown for the opening or closing of our ceremony.

Meanwhile, in 2006, I was awarded the Mountain State Bar Award for Outstanding Citizen. In addition, in 2006, I was the recipient of the West Virginia Bar Foundation Award for Public Citizen of the Year.

That award honors a West Virginian who has performed outstanding community service. And I was delighted to receive both of those awards.

Likewise, as a member of the West Virginia House of Delegates, I have had some remarkable opportunities. Once, I was asked by the Speaker of the West Virginia House of Delegates whether I could escort Governor Manchin, which he was at that time, up to the podium. He was there to give the State of the State address. And as we approached the podium, I exclaimed, "Good luck! I know you're going to make us proud."

He smiled. Then, he proceeded to the podium. Later, my daughter Gwen told me she heard me tell Governor Manchin, "I know you're going to make us proud."

I responded, "You did?"

She affirmed, "The entire state did. His microphone was on."

I just laughed. I thought, *I'm glad that is all I said*. Hence, I will never forget that moment.

Additionally, I had the honor of introducing Senator Barack Obama as he entered the reception for the Democratic fundraiser he had been invited to by Senator Robert Byrd. The reception was before the Jefferson-Jackson Dinner, and Senator Barack Obama was the keynote speaker for that event. However, as he was coming into the reception, he was immediately approached by a crowd of people.

I thought, *I should get down there and get my picture taken with him before he gets lost in the crowd.*

But when I went to go meet him, I was quite loquacious and said, "I have been talking and forgot to introduce myself."

He declared, "I know who you are! I understand you're running for office, and everyone says you're going to win." I smiled. I was amazed he knew who I was and that I was up for reelection in the West Virginia House of Delegates. That was truly an unforgettable occasion. I was fortunate to see Senator Barack Obama at another event before his presidency. I knew he was going to be in attendance, so I brought the picture we had taken at the prior event with me for him to sign. I wasn't going to miss the chance to have an autographed photo of Senator Barack Obama.

Moreover, in July of 2007, I received a phone call from a member of the Strong Men & Women in Virginia History award committee. She informed me that I had been nominated for the Strong Men & Women Award and asked me whether I would be attending the ceremony in Richmond, Virginia, or Cleveland, Ohio. I said, "I am not familiar with this award. Therefore, I will not be attending the ceremony."

She continued to say, "This is a very prestigious award, as many celebrities have been nominated for it."

I said, "That is making me more nervous about the award. I'm still not interested."

So after I hung up the phone with her, a few minutes later, a secretary for the West Virginia House of Delegates called me. She said, "The member of the Strong Men & Women award committee initially called me, and I gave her your phone number. And she just called me back and told me you are not going to attend the ceremony. So I told her to call you back in ten minutes."

I began to think, *Why did she tell her that?* Then, she began to convince me why I should attend the ceremony and accept the award. When the member of the Strong Men & Women award committee called back, I accepted the invitation to receive the Strong Men & Women Award in Cleveland, Ohio. I figured since I had a lot of family in Ohio, that would be the best place.

Afterward, I told Rogers, "If I go to Cleveland to receive this award, you have to go with me."

He responded, "OK." I was thinking, *He is just saying that. When it gets close to time, he is going to ask someone else to go in his place.* Because Rogers didn't like to travel.

However, he had been sick for a while, although I didn't realize how sick he was. The Strong Men & Women award ceremony was in February of 2008. Unfortunately, Rogers passed away in January 2008, a week before the ceremony. I was in agonizing pain. I can't begin to explain how heartbroken I was. Rogers and I had been married for fifty-six years when he passed. He was my lifelong best friend. We raised three beautiful children together. And Rogers worked so diligently on my campaigns by putting up my campaign signs and taking them all down on election day before the polls closed. I missed him so much. But with the love and support from family and friends, I persevered.

Rogers's funeral ceremony was held at Kingdom EMC Church, and Pastor Cain delivered the eulogy. And the church was full. To this day, I still hear from people that attended the funeral, they say that they'll never forget it. They say you aren't supposed to have fun at a funeral, but Pastor Cain did such a wonderful job delivering the eulogy that it didn't seem like a burial service.

Nevertheless, I still wasn't sure whether I was going to attend the Strong Men & Women award ceremony. And I hadn't had much time to think about it, being busy with Rogers's funeral arrangements. In addition, I was still mourning his loss.

However, I had already committed myself to be present at the Strong Men & Women award ceremony. Also, the gentleman who had nominated me for the award worked for Hope Gas Company, which is the company that runs the Strong Men & Women in Virginia History awards program. And he was picking me up and driving me to Cleveland, Ohio.

Furthermore, when he arrived, he proceeded to tell me the reason why he had nominated me for the award. He said he had observed me and noticed that I possess the leadership qualities for the Strong Men & Women Award. The Strong Men & Women Award honors African Americans, past and present, who have made notable contributions to their community and their professions. Wherefore, I was ecstatic and appreciative of my nomination.

Still, I have experienced being observed by others on numerous occasions. Additionally, I have received several job offers, been nominated for many awards, and been appointed to various positions because someone noticed the way in which I conduct myself and my distinctive characteristic traits. That's why I emphasize to people to be conscious of what they're doing and their surroundings because you never know who's watching you.

Moreover, the Strong Men & Women award ceremony was electrifying. It was by far one of the best award ceremonies I have ever attended. But more importantly, my family was there in great numbers. And I was so happy to see them. I am grateful to my family for always being there for me.

I represented the Fifty-first District in the West Virginia House of Delegates from 2004 to 2014. It was a great experience, and I felt really privileged to represent Monongalia County. I had been in office for a total of twenty-one years: seven years as mayor and fourteen years as a member of the West Virginia House of Delegates. *Now*, my journey was complete. So after fourteen years as a member of the West Virginia House of Delegates, I retired!

FINAL DESTINATION

SOMETIMES WHEN I THINK about all the things I've done, all the committees I've sat on, and all the positions I've held, it makes my head spin. As I had to overcome many obstacles during my journey. Additionally, I endured numerous tragedies and difficulties. But if I had to do it all over again, I wouldn't change my path! As I stated before, I didn't have a plan, but I believe somebody had a plan for me. And that plan helped me to move forward.

Even though I was born and raised in Osage, West Virginia, during segregation, I did not allow my circumstances to predict my aptitude. As there were many disadvantages I had to overcome. In addition, I experienced discrimination in high school, in college, at work, and in my political career. But I did not let it defeat me, especially since that was the intention.

I stayed focused on what I was proceeding to do, and whether it was becoming a member of the West Virginia Women's Board of Directors, becoming the vice president of the West Virginia Women's Bowling Association, running for Morgantown City Council, becoming the mayor of Morgantown, or becoming a member of the West Virginia House of

Delegates, I didn't deviate from my path. As a result, I was viewed as instrumental in my community, as well as appreciated by West Virginia University.

In January of 2015, I received a phone call from WVU president E. Gordon Gee. He informed me that I had been selected to receive an honorary doctor of laws degree during the 2015 West Virginia University commencement ceremony. I was *speechless*. This was another rare occasion when I was without words. However, eventually, I said, "I'm honored. I'll be delighted to receive the degree."

So in May of 2015, WVU awarded five special degrees among the 4,500 diplomas that were presented during the commencement ceremony. And I was the recipient of one of those special degrees, as I received an honorary doctor of laws degree. It was a momentous occasion, considering that I wasn't allowed to attend WVU during segregation and now they were awarding me with an honorary doctor of laws degree. Hence, I will always be grateful for the experience.

Moreover, my family attended the ceremony, and I am appreciative of them for that. I am thankful for all my family, all my old friends, and all the new friends I made along the way. I can't thank them enough for their support. For instance, one couple, in particular, is Kenny Jackson and Diana Lewis Jackson. They are very good friends of mine. Additionally, Kenny is always available to assist me with things around my house. He knows my son is in Ohio, so he takes the place of my son not being here and helps me out. I am truly blessed that Kenny Jackson and Diana Lewis Jackson are a part of my family.

Therefore, my life has been phenomenal, even with the obstacles. Everything I learned during my journey prepared me for my destination! I used to think that certain things were only for certain people because of the era I grew up in. I thought certain things were for them and certain things were for me. And that was just the way it was. However, I've realized that is *not* the way it is. If I work hard enough, I can succeed and obtain those same things. Wherefore, if you do more than just the ordinary, you too can have an extraordinary life!

THE END!

ABOUT THE AUTHOR

Vonnetta Mayo was born in Gary, Indiana, and raised in Southern California. She then relocated to the Sunshine State, Florida. However, afterward, she lived in Morgantown, West Virginia, for a couple of years. Now, she resides in New Bremen, Ohio.

Vonnetta Mayo is the youngest of four children. At an early age, she aspired to become a writer. Vonnetta Mayo's mother and father both were influential in her becoming a writer. She started writing poems for church conventions. And as a teenager, Vonnetta Mayo won an essay contest and received a scholarship for college. Then, at the University of California, San Diego, she minored in literature and writing. That is where her goal of becoming a writer emerged.

Vonnetta Mayo loves God and attributes her inspiration for writing to God. She was raised in the church. That is where she acquired most of her teachings and beliefs. She believes in pursuing and never giving up on your dreams. Therefore, Vonnetta Mayo is the proud author of a two-book series, *Joy in Sorrow, Hope for Tomorrow* and *Joy in Sorrow, Hope for Tomorrow: Homecoming*. She thanks God for making her dream of becoming an author come true.